THE *Missing* SHOP MANUAL

BAND SAW

BAND SAW

{ the tool information you need at your fingertips }

skills institute
press

Distributed by
Fox Chapel Publishing

FOX CHAPEL
PUBLISHING

© 2010 by Skills Institute Press LLC
"Missing Shop Manual" series trademark of Skills Institute Press
Published and distributed in North America by Fox Chapel Publishing Company, Inc.

Band Saw is an original work, first published in 2010.

Portions of text and art previously published by and reproduced under license with Direct Holdings Americas Inc.

ISBN 978-1-56523-492-5

Library of Congress Cataloging-in-Publication Data

Band Saw.

    p. cm. -- (The missing shop manual)

Includes index.

ISBN 978-1-56523-492-5

1. Band saws. I. Fox Chapel Publishing.

TT186.B287 2010

684'.083--dc22

2010016958

To learn more about the other great books from Fox Chapel Publishing, or to find a retailer near you, call toll-free 800-457-9112 or visit us at *www.FoxChapelPublishing.com*.

Note to Authors: We are always looking for talented authors to write new books in our area of woodworking, design, and related crafts. Please send a brief letter describing your idea to Acquisition Editor, 1970 Broad Street, East Petersburg, PA 17520.

Printed in China
First printing: November 2010

Contents

WHAT YOU WILL LEARN

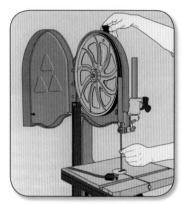

Chapter 1:
Band Saw, page 8

Chapter 2:
Band Saw Blades, page 32

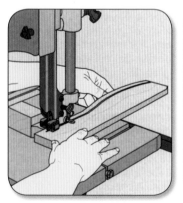

Chapter 3:
Cutting Curves, page 46

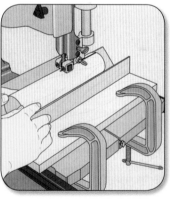

Chapter 4:
Straight Cuts, page 60

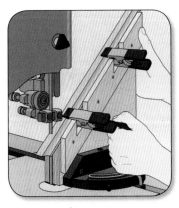

Chapter 5:
Cutting Duplicate Pieces, page 74

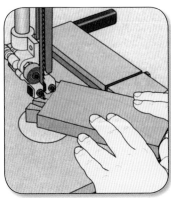

Chapter 6:
Band Saw Joinery, page 88

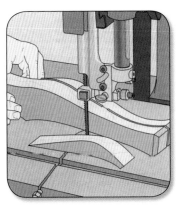

Chapter 7:
Cabriole Legs, page 100

Band Saw

For ease of operation and wide-ranging utility, the band saw is hard to beat. It is the only woodworking machine capable of making both straight and contour cuts. In addition to crosscutting and ripping, it is well suited for cutting curves and circles, enabling the woodworker to produce anything from a dovetail joint to a cabriole leg.

Both rough and delicate work fall within its domain. Fitted with a ½-inch blade—the widest size available for most consumer-grade machines—a band saw can resaw 6-inch-thick lumber into two thinner pieces in a single pass. And with a ¹⁄₁₆-inch blade, a band saw can zigzag its way through a board at virtually any angle, even making 90° turns during a cut. Many cuts can be made freehand by simply pivoting the workpiece around the blade. With the cutting techniques and shop-made jigs presented in this

This quarter-circle-cutting jig is an ideal time-saver for rounding corners for tabletops. The jig pivots around a fixed point, taking the guesswork out of cutting perfect arcs.

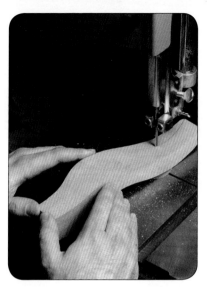

A ¼-inch band saw blade weaves its way along a curved cutting line, paring away a block of mahogany to form a graceful cabriole leg.

chapter, you will be able to turn out intricate curves, cut perfect circles, and produce uniformly square-edged rip cuts and crosscuts.

Compared to the radial arm saw or table saw, the band saw is a quiet machine, so noise-related fatigue is rarely a problem. Moreover, very little of the blade—usually only ⅛ inch—is ever exposed while it is running. And since the cutting action of the blade bears down on the workpiece, pushing it against the table instead of back toward the operator, kickback cannot occur. For this reason, the band saw is the tool of choice for ripping short or narrow stock.

Band saws are classified according to their throat width, which supports the machine's upper wheel. Band saws for home workshops fall in the 10- to 14-inch range. Saws are also categorized according to their depth-of-cut capacity, which corresponds to the maximum gap between the table and the upper guide assembly. In choosing a band saw, look for one with a sturdy table that can tilt 45° in one direction and at least 10° in the other. In addition, consider spending a little more for a ¾-horsepower motor.

ANATOMY OF A BAND SAW

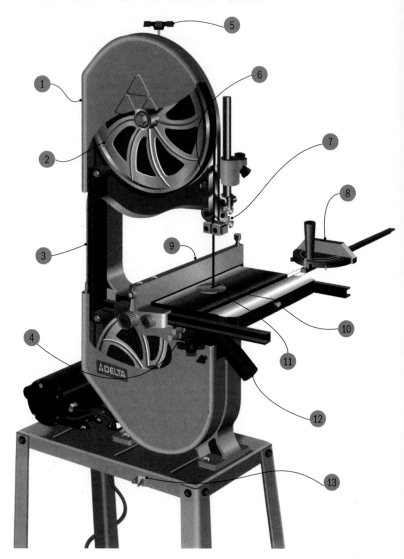

1. Wheel cover
Protects operator from wheel and blade; may be removable or hinged to provide access to wheel.

2. Wheel
Rimmed by a rubber tire that cushions the blade and keeps it from slipping.

3. Throat column
Supports blade between wheels and protects operator from blade.

4. Table lock knob
Allows table to be tilted for bevel or compound cuts; a second knob is located on opposite side of table.

5. Tension handle
Raises and lowers upper wheel to adjust blade tension.

6. Blade guard
Protects operator from blade; moved up and down with guide assembly.

7. Upper guide assembly
Raised and lowered depending on thickness of workpiece; includes blade guard, thrust bearing and guide blocks. Setscrews release guide blocks for lateral adjustment; thumbscrews release bearing and blocks for front-to-back adjustment by means of adjusting knobs. (A fixed guide assembly with thrust bearing and guide blocks is located under table insert.)

8. Miter gauge
Guides workpiece across table for crosscuts or miter cuts.

9. Rip fence
Guides workpiece across table for rip cuts, crosscuts and resawing.

10. Table leveling pin
Adjustable to keep miter gauge slot properly aligned.

11. Table insert
Prevents wood pieces from falling into table and supports workpiece when close to blade; usually made of aluminum.

12. Dust spout
For dust collection system.

13. On/Off switch
Can be padlocked in off position for safety.

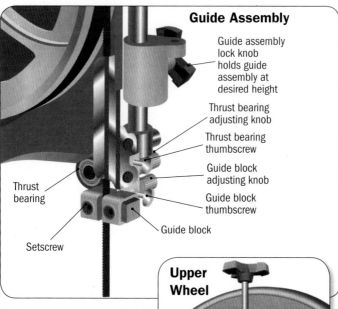

Guide Assembly

Guide assembly lock knob holds guide assembly at desired height

Thrust bearing adjusting knob

Thrust bearing thumbscrew

Guide block adjusting knob

Guide block thumbscrew

Thrust bearing

Guide block

Setscrew

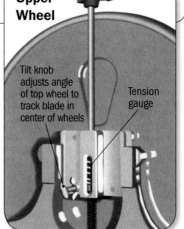

Upper Wheel

Tilt knob adjusts angle of top wheel to track blade in center of wheels

Tension gauge

As the name suggests, a band saw blade is a continuous steel band. Varying in length from roughly 72 inches to 104 inches depending on the size of the machine, the blade runs around rubber-rimmed wheels and passes through an opening in the saw table. One of the wheels—typically the lower one—is the drive wheel, which is turned by a motor. The blade is not fastened to the wheels but is held in place by tension and turns through its elliptical

ANATOMY OF A BAND SAW *(continued)*

The three-wheel band saw's wide throat capacity—typically 20 inches, rather than the 10 to 14 inches available on most two-wheel models—makes it more convenient for working with particularly large workpieces.

path at roughly 3,000 feet per minute—the average cutting speed for a 14-inch saw.

The blade is kept taut by means of a tension handle, which raises and lowers the upper wheel. A tilt knob that cants the upper wheel is used to keep the blade centered on the wheels. The blade is kept steady on its path by thrust bearings located behind the blade above and below the table, and by guide blocks, which prevent lateral movement. Although some cuts can be made freehand, a rip fence and miter gauge are available with many models to guide workpieces across the table.

SETTING UP

The band saw has a reputation among some woodworkers as a relatively imprecise cutting tool. And yet, band saws are routinely used in industry to cut very hard materials such as metal to very close tolerances. The fact remains, however, that the tool can only be made to cut straight edges and precise curves if it is kept finely tuned.

The ideal is for the blade to cut squarely into the workpiece, producing a smooth, accurate result. But the peculiarities of band saw geometry can make this ideal difficult to achieve. After bending around the machine's wheels at 35 miles per hour, a section of the blade must straighten out by the time it reaches the saw table a split second later.

For this to happen, the adjustable parts of the saw must be kept in proper alignment so the blade runs smoothly and square to the table. Particular attention should be paid to the wheels, the guide assembly and the saw table itself.

To tune your band saw, unplug it, install and tension the blade you plan to use *(page 23),* then follow the setup steps detailed on the following pages. Take the time to do it right. Adjusting the band saw may be more time-consuming than learning how to operate the tool. But the advantages of a well-tuned machine will be noticeable not only in the quality of the results but also in the longevity of your blades and of the band saw itself. Misaligned wheels or poorly adjusted guide blocks can lead to premature blade wear or breakage.

Installing nonmetallic guide blocks on a band saw can reduce wear and tear appreciably *(page 27),* but there is no substitute for checking thrust bearings, guide blocks and wheels for proper alignment.

ALIGNING THE WHEELS

Checking wheel alignment

To make certain that the wheels are parallel to each other and in the same vertical plane, loosen the table lock knobs and tilt the table out of the way. Open both wheel covers and hold a long straightedge against the wheel rims as shown. The straightedge should rest flush against the top and bottom of each wheel.

If the wheels are out of alignment, try to bring the top wheel to a vertical position by means of the tilt knob. If the straightedge still will not rest flush, you will have to adjust the position of the upper wheel.

Shifting the upper wheel

Move the upper wheel in or out on its axle following the instructions in your owner's manual. On the model shown, you must first remove the blade *(page 22)* and the wheel. Then shift the wheel by either adding or removing one or more washers *(right)*. Reinstall the wheel and tighten the axle nut. Install the blade and recheck wheel alignment.

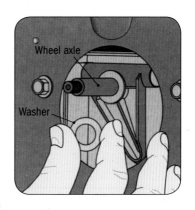

Wheel axle

Washer

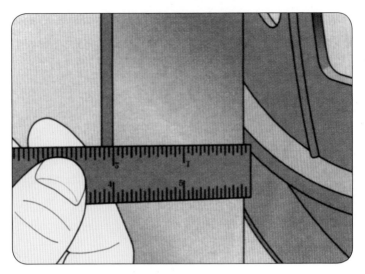

Rechecking wheel alignment

If the straightedge still will not rest flush, measure the gap between the recessed wheel and the straightedge *(above)* to determine how far you need to move the outermost wheel in.

ALIGNING THE WHEELS *(continued)*

Shifting the outermost wheel into alignment

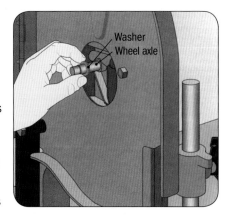

Washer
Wheel axle

Remove the outermost wheel following the instructions in your owner's manual. (It is better to shift the outermost wheel in to correct the alignment rather than to move the inner wheel out; this keeps the wheels as close as possible to the saw frame.) Then shift the wheel by removing one or more of the factory-installed washers *(above)*. (If there are no washers, you can shim the recessed wheel with washers to bring the wheels into alignment.) Reinstall the wheel and tighten the axle nut. Recheck wheel alignment.

---

*Shop*Tip

Balancing a band saw wheel
To check the wheels of a band saw for balance, spin each one by hand. When it comes to rest, make a mark at the bottom and spin it again. If the mark comes to rest at the bottom more than two times out of three, the wheel is imbalanced. To correct the problem, drill shallow holes between the rim and spokes at the heavy point *(right)*. Remount the wheel and perform the test again. Bore as many holes as necessary. When the wheel stops returning to the same position, it is balanced.

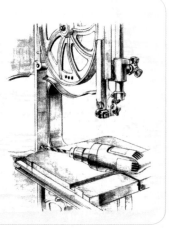

BAND SAWS

For many woodworkers, the band saw's thin, flexible blade makes it the tool of choice for cutting curves, resawing, and making fine, straight cuts. And because the blade teeth cut downward, there is no danger of kickback.

Since the band saw blade is supported only on the crown of two large wheels, it must be properly tensioned and tracked *(page 24)* every time you change blades; otherwise you risk crooked cuts and broken blades. Setup adjustments for the machine are not time-consuming, but they are important. Particular attention should be paid to the alignment of the wheels *(page 16)*. Misaligned wheels can cause excessive blade vibration. Also, periodically adjust the guide assemblies and check the table for square *(page 26)*.

After many hours of use, the tires on band saw wheels can become worn, caked with sawdust, or stretched out of shape. If the thickness of a band saw tire is uneven around the wheel, inserting a screwdriver blade under the tire, as shown in the photo above, and working it around the tire's circumference can restore its proper shape.

If these procedures do not restore a poorly cutting saw to peak performance, the wheels or tires may be to blame. The steps shown on the following pages detail how to correct out-of-round and unbalanced wheels, and will make your band saw cut straighter and help its blades last longer.

CHECKING THE WHEELS

Checking the wheel bearings

Open one wheel cover, grasp the wheel at the sides and rock it back and forth *(above)*. Repeat while holding the wheel at the top and bottom. If there is play in the wheel or you hear a clunking noise, remove the wheel and replace the bearing. Then repeat the test for the other wheel.

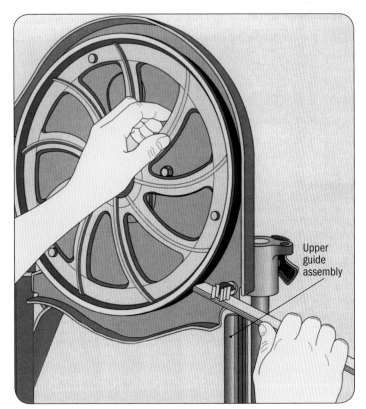

Upper
guide
assembly

Testing for out-of-round wheels

Start with the upper wheel. Bracing a stick against the upper guide assembly, hold the end of the stick about ¹⁄₁₆ inch away from the wheel's tire. Then spin the wheel by hand *(above)*. If the wheel or tire is out of round, the gap between the stick and the wheel will fluctuate; the wheel may even hit the stick. If the discrepancy exceeds ¹⁄₃₂ inch, remedy the problem. Repeat the test for the lower wheel.

CHECKING THE WHEELS *(continued)*

Fixing an out-of-round wheel

Start by determining whether the tire or the wheel itself is the problem. Try stretching the tire into shape with a screwdriver, then repeat the previous test. If the wheel is still out of round, use a sanding block to sand the tire; this may compensate for uneveness in the tire. For the lower wheel, turn on the saw and hold the sanding block against the spinning tire *(above)*. For the upper wheel, leave the saw unplugged and rotate the wheel by hand. Retest. If the problem persists, the wheel itself is out of round. Have it trued at a machinist's shop.

CHANGING A SAW BLADE

Removing the old blade

Raise the upper guide assembly to its highest setting and lock it in place. Back the thrust bearings and guide blocks away from the blade *(page 26)*. Remove the table insert and use locking pliers to remove the table leveling pin. Turn the tension handle counterclockwise to release the blade tension, then open the wheel covers. Wearing safety goggles, carefully slide the blade out of the guide assemblies *(right)*, then slip it off the wheels and guide it through the table slot.

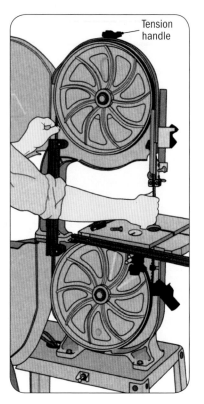

Tension handle

CHANGING A SAW BLADE *(continued)*

Installing the new blade

If the blade is coiled, uncoil it carefully. Band saw blades store a considerable amount of spring. Wearing safety goggles and gloves, hold the blade at arm's length in one hand and turn your face away as the blade uncoils. Guide the blade through the table slot as shown, holding it with the teeth facing you and pointing down. Slip the blade between the guide blocks and in the throat column slot, then center it on the wheels. Install the leveling pin and table insert. Tension and track the blade *(page 24)*.

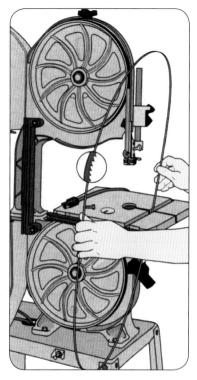

TENSIONING AND TRACKING A BLADE

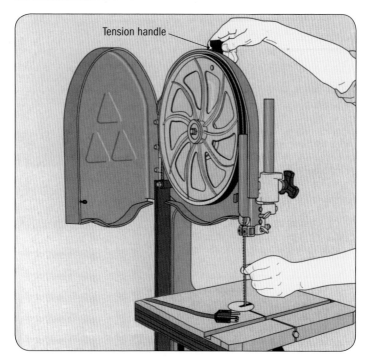

Tension handle

Tensioning a blade

Turn the tension handle clockwise with one hand to raise the top wheel and increase tension on the blade; deflect the blade from side to side with the other hand to gauge the tension. Spin the upper wheel by hand and gauge the tension at several points along the blade. Increase the tension *(above)* until the blade deflects about ¼ inch to either side of the vertical position. Avoid overtensioning a blade; this can lead to premature blade wear and breakage. Undertensioning a blade will allow it to wander back and forth and side to side as it cuts.

TENSIONING AND TRACKING
A BLADE *(continued)*

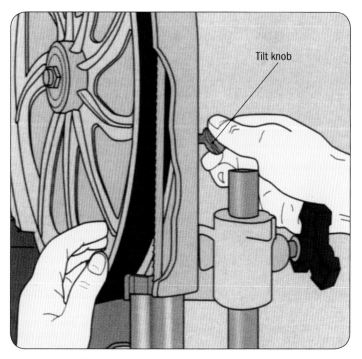

Tilt knob

Tracking a blade

Lower the upper guide assembly, then spin the upper wheel by hand to check whether the blade is tracking in the center of the wheel. If it is not, loosen the tilt knob lock screw. Then, spin the wheel with one hand while turning the tilt knob with the other hand *(above)* to angle the wheel until the blade tracks in the center. To check the tracking, close the wheel covers and turn on the saw, then turn it off; adjust the tracking, if necessary. Set the thrust bearings and guide blocks *(page 26)*.

ADJUSTING THE GUIDE ASSEMBLIES

Setting the thrust bearings

Set the upper guide assembly, then check by eye that the upper thrust bearing is square to the blade. If not, loosen the guide assembly setscrew, adjust the assembly so the bearing is square to the blade, and tighten the

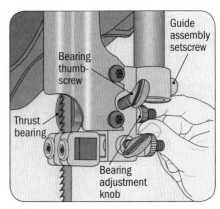

setscrew. Then, loosen the bearing thumbscrew and turn the adjustment knob until the bearing just touches the blade. Back the bearing off slightly *(above)* and tighten the thumbscrew. (The lower thrust bearing, which is located directly under the table insert, is adjusted the same way.) To check the setting, spin the upper wheel by hand. If the blade makes either bearing spin, back the bearing off slightly and recheck.

Setting the guide blocks

To set the upper guide blocks, loosen the guide block setscrews and pinch the blocks together using your thumb and index finger until they almost touch the blade. Alternatively, use a slip

ADJUSTING THE
GUIDE ASSEMBLIES *(continued)*

of paper to set the space between the blocks and the blade. Tighten the setscrews. Next, loosen the thumbscrew and turn the adjustment knob until the front edges of the guide blocks are just behind the blade gullets *(opposite, bottom)*. Tighten the thumbscrew. Set the lower guide blocks the same way.

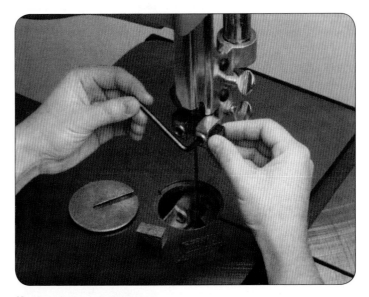

Heat-resistant guide blocks

Designed to replace the metal guide blocks supplied with most saws, nonmetallic blocks are made from a graphite-impregnated resin that contains a dry lubricant. Because they build up less heat than conventional guide blocks, the nonmetallic variety last longer; they can also be set closer to the blade, promoting more accurate and controlled cuts. In addition, contact between the blade and nonmetallic blocks does not dull the blade, as is common with metal blocks. To install, unscrew the guide block setscrews, remove the old blocks and replace with the new blocks; tighten the setscrews.

SQUARING THE TABLE AND BLADE

Aligning the table

To ensure that the miter gauge slot is properly aligned on both sides of the table slot, set the miter gauge in its slot and slide the gauge back and forth across the table. The gauge should slide

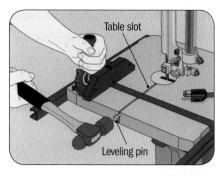

Table slot

Leveling pin

freely with only moderate pressure. If the gauge binds, use locking pliers to remove the leveling pin. Then, insert the pin into its hole and use a ball-peen hammer to tap the pin deeper *(above)* until the miter gauge slides freely.

Checking the table angle

With the table in the horizontal position, remove the table insert, then butt a combination square against the saw blade as shown. The square should fit flush against the saw blade. If there is a gap between the two, loosen the two table lock knobs and make sure

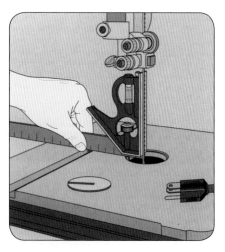

the table is seated properly on the table stop under the table. Tighten the lock knobs. If the gap remains, adjust the table stop.

SQUARING THE
TABLE AND BLADE *(continued)*

Adjusting the table stop

Tilt the table out of the way, then use two wrenches as shown to adjust the table stop. Use the lower wrench to hold the nut stationary and the upper wrench to turn the table stop: clockwise to lower it, counterclockwise to raise it. Recheck the table angle.

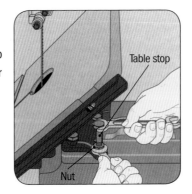

Table stop

Nut

BAND SAW SAFETY TIPS

- Except when changing a blade, always keep the wheel covers closed.

- Make sure that saw blades are sharp, clean, and undamaged. Disconnect the saw before changing a blade.

- Stand slightly to the left of the blade when cutting at the front of the band saw table. Do not stand, or allow anyone else to stand, to the right of the blade. This is the direction in which the blade will fly if it breaks.

- Do not cut until the blade is turning at full speed.

- Keep your hands away from the blade when the saw is on. Use a push stick or a jig to cut small or narrow pieces.

- Avoid making turns that are too tight for the blade you are using. This can break the blade.

- Cut with the blade guard no more than ⅛ inch above the workpiece.

- Before backing out of a cut, turn off the saw.

SAFETY

Compared to the table saw or radial arm saw, the band saw seems a relatively safe machine. There is no aggressive whine of a 1½- or 3-horse-power motor turning a 10-inch saw blade; instead, the band saw produces a quiet hum that some woodworkers liken to the sound of a sewing machine. And with its blade guard properly set, no more than ⅛ inch of the blade is exposed above the table.

Still, it is impossible to be too careful with any woodworking machine, and the band saw is no exception. Band saw blades occasionally break, and when they do they tend to fly to the right of where the operator normally stands. Therefore, it is wise to stand slightly to the throat column side of the blade whenever possible. If a blade snaps, turn off the saw and do not open the wheel covers to install a new blade until the wheels have stopped completely.

Although the blade guard adequately covers the blade above the table, there is no guard at the level of the table or underneath it. As a result, you need to keep your hands out of the hole covered by the table insert and refrain from reaching under the table to clear debris from the blade before the blade has come to a stop.

Most of the accidents that occur with the band saw are a result of excessive feed pressure and poor hand position. Feed a workpiece steadily into the blade, but with a minimal amount of pressure, or the blade may jam and break. For most cuts, feed the workpiece with one hand, using the other hand to guide it. Keep your fingers out of line with the blade. Hook the fingers of the feed hand around an edge of the workpiece to prevent them from slipping into the blade as your hand nears the cutting area.

CUTTING SAFELY WITH THE BAND SAW

Setting the upper guide assembly and blade guard

Before turning on the saw to begin a cut, set the upper guide assembly ⅛ inch above the workpiece. Use one hand to hold the guide assembly in position and the other hand to tighten the guide assembly lock knob *(right)*. Alternatively, use

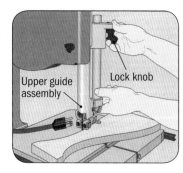

Upper guide assembly

Lock knob

the workpiece to lever the guide assembly up slightly, then tighten the lock knob. Setting the guide assembly as close to the workpiece as possible does not only protect you from the blade when the saw is running; it also supports the blade as it cuts, minimizing excessive blade deflection.

DUST HOODS

Connecting a dust collection system to tools with dust ports

Use a commercial adapter to attach a collection hose to a machine dust port. The adapter should be sized to friction-fit the collection hose at one end and slip over the dust port at the other, as shown on the band saw *(right)*. For the radial arm saw, a hose clamp is used for reinforcement.

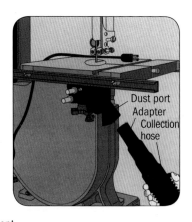

Dust port

Adapter

Collection hose

Band Saw Blades

Lumber mill band saws regularly use blades as wide as 12 inches to cut logs into boards. Blades for consumer-grade saws are much smaller—generally ranging from ¹⁄₁₆ to ½ inch wide. But even within this relatively narrow spectrum, choosing the best blade for the job is not always straightforward.

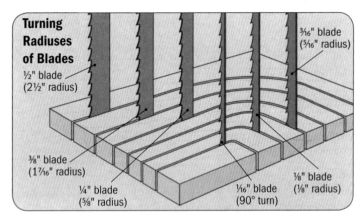

Turning Radiuses of Blades

½" blade (2½" radius)

³⁄₁₆" blade (⁵⁄₁₆" radius)

³⁄₈" blade (1⁷⁄₁₆" radius)

¼" blade (⁵⁄₈" radius)

¹⁄₁₆" blade (90° turn)

⅛" blade (⅛" radius)

When choosing a band saw blade for a contour cut, consider the tightest curve that the blade will turn. Use the chart above as a rough guide. In general, the narrower the blade, the tighter the curve, given the same blade set. But because wider blades resist unwanted deflection, a narrow blade is not always the best choice for a curved cut. A good rule of thumb is to use the widest blade for the tightest curve required. The limitations on a blade's turning capacity cannot be ignored. Forcing a blade around a corner that is too tight will cause it to bind in the kerf, twist, and ultimately snap.

There is no single all-purpose combination blade in band sawing, nor any blade specifically designed for ripping or crosscutting. However, a woodworker should keep three basic variables in mind: tooth design, blade width, and blade set.

As illustrated on page 35, band saw blades for cutting wood are available in three basic tooth designs; each design does something better than the others. The chart at left shows the importance of selecting a blade of appropriate width for cutting curves. In general, narrow blades are used for cuts with intricate curves, while wide blades are ideal for resawing thick stock.

Blade set refers to how much the blade teeth are angled to the side, making a saw cut—or kerf—that is wider than the blade. This reduces the chance of the blade binding in a cut. A blade with minimal set, called a light set blade, produces a smooth cut and a narrow kerf, but is also more prone to binding, which limits its ability to cut a tight curve. A heavy set blade—one with greater set—cuts faster than a light set blade, and is less likely to bind due to its wider kerf. However, a heavy set blade leaves more visible corrugated marks in the cut edge of a workpiece, an effect called "washboarding."

The typical band saw blade has a loop length of several feet. To reduce the amount of storage space, fold the blade into three loops as shown on page 44. Clean a band saw blade regularly to keep it from gumming up with resins and pitch. Use a wire or stiff-bristled brush dipped in solvent such as turpentine, oven cleaner, or an ammonia-based cleaner. Before storing a blade or for removing rust, wipe the blade with an oily rag. For rust, use steel wool.

SHARPENING A BAND SAW BLADE

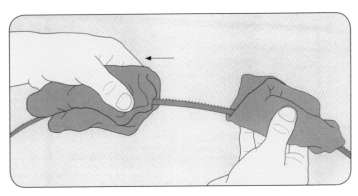

Cleaning the blade

Before sharpening a band saw blade, remove sawdust and wood chips from it. Make sure you release the blade tension first, before slipping the blade off the wheels. Then, holding the blade between two clean rags *(above)*, pull it away in the direction opposite its normal rotation to avoid snagging the cutting edges in the material.

Secured between two wood blocks in a bench vise, the teeth of a band saw blade are sharpened with a triangular file. Band saw blades can also be honed while they are installed on the machine. The teeth should be sharpened periodically and set after every three to five sharpenings. In fact, a properly honed and set band saw blade will perform better than a brand-new one.

SHARPENING A
BAND SAW BLADE *(continued)*

Blade Types

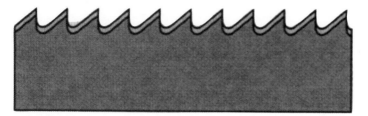

Standard Blade
For straight cuts across the grain or diagonal to the grain. Ideal for intricate curves or cuts when the orientation of the blade to the grain changes during the cut.

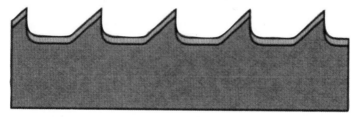

Skip-tooth Blade
So called because every other tooth is missing. For long, gentle curves with the grain. Cuts faster, but more roughly, than a standard blade. A ¼-inch skip-tooth blade with 4 to 6 teeth per inch is a good all-purpose blade.

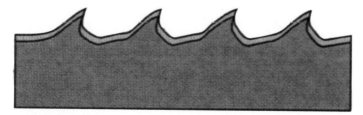

Hook-tooth Blade
For straight cuts and curves with the grain; the best blade for ripping or resawing.

SHARPENING A
BAND SAW BLADE *(continued)*

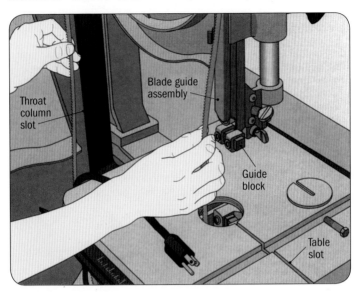

Throat
column
slot

Blade guide
assembly

Guide
block

Table
slot

Installing the blade for sharpening

You can sharpen a band saw blade either on a bench vise or on the
machine. To install the blade on the band saw for sharpening, mount it
with the teeth pointing opposite their cutting position—that is, facing up
instead of down. Turn the blade inside out and guide it through the table
slot *(above)*, holding it with the teeth facing you and pointing up. Slip
the blade between the guide blocks and in the throat column slot, then
center it on the wheels. Make sure the blade guide assembly is raised
as high above the table as it will go.

SHARPENING A
BAND SAW BLADE *(continued)*

Setting the blade

If the teeth need to be set, adjust a commercial saw set to the same number of teeth per inch as the band saw blade. Secure the blade in a handscrew and clamp the handscrew to the saw table. Starting at the handscrew end of

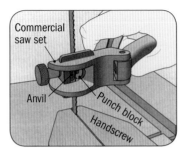

Commercial saw set

Anvil

Punch block

Handscrew

the blade, position the first tooth that is bent to the right between the anvil and punch block of the saw set and squeeze the handle to set the tooth *(above)*. Work your way up to the guide assembly, setting all the teeth that are bent to the right. Then turn the saw set over and repeat for the leftward-bent teeth. Continue setting all the blade teeth section by section. To ensure you do not omit any teeth, mark each section you work on with chalk.

Sharpening the blade

Sharpen the teeth the same way you set them, working on one blade section at a time. Hold a triangular file at a 90° angle to the blade and sharpen each tooth that is set to the right, guiding the file in the same direction that the tooth is set *(right)*. Then sharpen

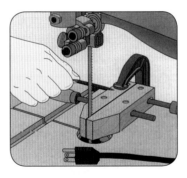

the leftward-bent teeth the same way. Use the same number of strokes on each tooth. Once all the teeth have been sharpened, remove the blade, turn it inside out and reinstall it for cutting, with the teeth pointing down. Tension and track the blade *(page 24.)*

SHARPENING A
BAND SAW BLADE *(continued)*

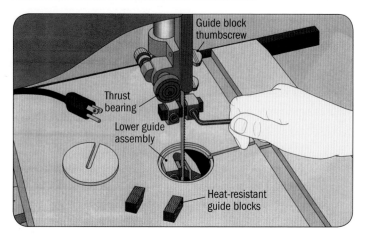

Guide block thumbscrew

Thrust bearing

Lower guide assembly

Heat-resistant guide blocks

Installing heat-resistant guide blocks

Replacing your band saw's standard guide blocks with heat-resistant blocks will lengthen blade life and promote more accurate and controlled cuts. Remove the original blocks by using a hex wrench to loosen the setscrews securing them to the upper guide assembly *(above)*. Slip out the old blocks and insert the replacements. Pinch the blocks together with your thumb and index finger until they almost touch the blade. (You can also use a slip of paper to set the space between the guide blocks and the blade). Tighten the setscrews. The front edges of the guide blocks should be just behind the blade gullets. To reposition the blocks, loosen their thumbscrew and turn their adjustment knob to advance or retract the blocks. Tighten the thumbscrew and repeat the process for the guide assembly located below the table.

SHARPENING A
BAND SAW BLADE *(continued)*

ShopTip

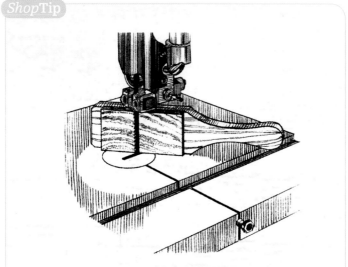

Rounding a band saw blade
To help prevent a new band saw blade from binding in the kerf of curved cuts, use a silicon-carbide stone without oil to round its back edge, as shown here. Attach the stone to a shop-made handle. Tension and track the blade *(page 24)*, then turn on the saw. Wearing safety goggles, hold the stone against the back of the blade and slowly pivot the stone. Turn off the saw after a few minutes. In addition to rounding the back of the blade, the stone will smooth any bumps where the blade ends are welded together.

REPAIRING A BROKEN BAND SAW BLADE

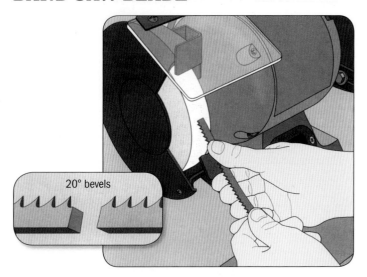

20° bevels

Grinding the broken ends of the blade

A broken band saw blade can be repaired in the shop. Start by creating a 20° bevel on each end of the blade using a bench grinder *(above)*. As shown in the inset, the bevels will increase the contact area between the two blade ends when you join them, strengthening the joint. Then use a piece of emery cloth to roughen both blade ends; sand the surfaces until their bluish color disappears. This will help the soldering alloy adhere to the blade surface properly.

REPAIRING A BROKEN
BAND SAW BLADE *(continued)*

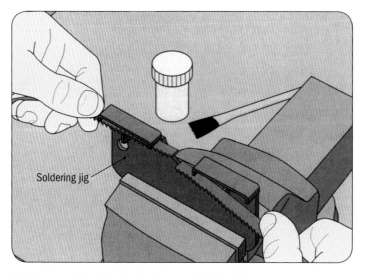

Soldering jig

Setting up the blade in the soldering jig

Secure a commercial soldering jig in a machinist's vise. Next, use a brush to spread flux on the beveled ends of the blade and ½ inch in from each end. Position the blade in the jig so the two beveled ends are in contact *(above)*. Make sure the blade is tight and straight in the jig.

REPAIRING A BROKEN
BAND SAW BLADE *(continued)*

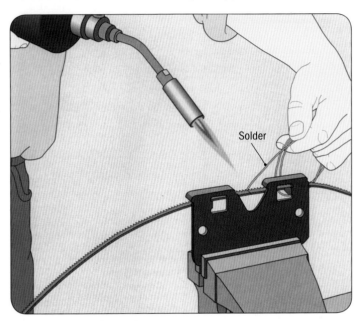

Solder

Soldering the blade ends

Heat the joint with a propane torch, then unroll a length of the solder and touch the tip to the joint—not to the flame. Continue heating the joint *(above)* until the solder covers the joint completely. Turn off the torch and let the joint cool.

REPAIRING A BROKEN
BAND SAW BLADE *(continued)*

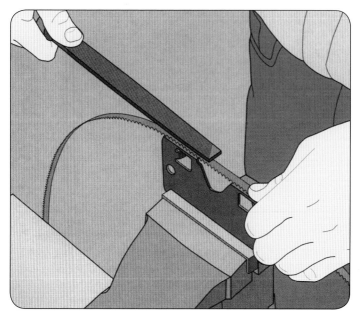

Filing the joint

Once the joint has cooled, remove the blade from the jig and wash off the flux with warm water. If there is an excess of solder on the blade, file it off carefully with a single-cut bastard mill file *(above)* until the joint is no thicker than the rest of the blade. If the joint separates, reheat it to melt the solder, pull it apart, and repeat previous steps.

FOLDING AND STORING A BAND SAW BLADE

Holding the blade

Before storing a band saw blade, remove any rust from it with steel wool and wipe it with an oily rag. Then, wearing safety goggles and gloves, grasp the blade with the teeth facing away from you; point your left thumb up and your right thumb down *(right)*.

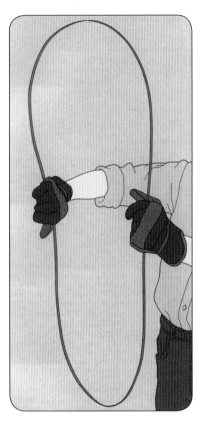

FOLDING AND STORING A BAND SAW BLADE *(continued)*

Twisting the blade

Pressing your right thumb firmly against the blade, twist it by pivoting your right hand upward. The blade will begin to form two loops *(right)*.

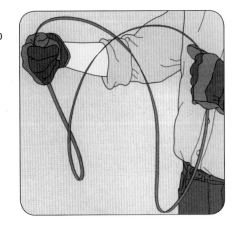

Coiling the blade

Without pausing or releasing the blade, keep rotating it in the same direction while pivoting your left hand in the opposite direction. The blade will coil again, forming a third loop *(right)*. Secure the blade with string, pipe cleaners, or plastic twist ties.

Cutting Curves

Much of the curved wood that graces well-made furniture is cut on the band saw, which can produce virtually any contour. As shown in the pages that follow, you cut curves in a variety of ways: by sawing freehand along a cutting line, by making use of a pattern *(page 49)* or by relying on shop-built jigs.

Whatever the shape of the curve, the biggest challenge in contour-cutting is avoiding dead ends, where the workpiece hits the throat column before the end of a cut. When this occurs, you have to veer off the cutting line and saw to the edge of the workpiece, or turn off the saw and back the blade out of the cut. In either case, you must choose a new starting point for the cut. The key to avoiding such pitfalls is to visualize the cut before you make it so you can select the best starting point.

Using a band saw and a shop-made circle-cutting jig like the one shown on page 58, a woodworker cut the top of this Shaker-style table. The table's legs were also produced on the band saw.

CUTTING A CURVE FREEHAND

Making release cuts and starting the curved cut

To keep the blade from binding in the kerf of a curved cut, make a series of straight release cuts from the edge of the workpiece to the cutting line. The exact location of the cuts is arbitrary, but try to make them to the tightest parts of

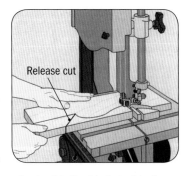

Release cut

the curve, as shown. To start the curved cut, align the blade just to the waste side of the cutting line. Feed the workpiece steadily into the blade using your right hand, while guiding it with your left hand *(above)*. Make sure that neither hand is in line with the blade.

Finishing the cut

To cut the tightest parts of the curve, pivot the workpiece on the table, shifting your hand position as necessary. For the cut shown, saw to the end of the curved portion of the cutting line, feeding with your left hand. Pivot the workpiece with your right hand to

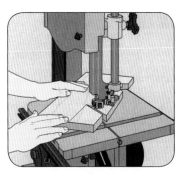

avoid twisting the blade; veer off the cutting line and saw to a release cut, if necessary. Keep two fingers of your right hand braced against the table to maintain control of the cut *(above)*. Turn the workpiece around and cut along the straight portion of the cutting line.

MAKING MULTIPLE CURVED CUTS

Setting up the fence and starting the cut

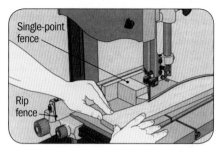

To produce multiple curved pieces with the same width from a single workpiece, cut the first curve freehand *(page 47)*. Then, make a T-shaped single-point fence

with a rounded nose at the base of the T. Cut a notch in the base so that the guide assembly can be lowered to the workpiece. (Note: In this illustration, the guide assembly is raised for clarity.) Install the rip fence and screw the single-point fence to it with the tip of the base parallel to the blade. Position the rip fence for the width of cut. To start each cut, butt the workpiece against the tip of the single-point fence and feed it into the blade using both hands *(above)*. Keep the workpiece square to the tip of the single-point fence and ensure that neither hand is in line with the blade.

Finishing the cut

As the trailing end of the workpiece nears the tip of the single-point fence, shift your left hand to the back of the table to support the cut piece. Brace your left arm on the fence and hook two fingers over the edge of the table to keep your arm clear of the blade *(right)*. Continue feeding with your right hand until the cut is completed.

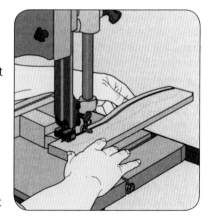

PATTERN SAWING

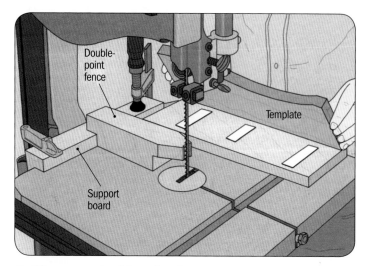

Double-point fence

Template

Support board

Setting up a double-point fence

To cut the same curved pattern from different workpieces, cut the first piece freehand *(page 47)*; then, use it as a template to cut the other pieces. Prepare a double-point fence with a shallow notch at the end for the blade and a deeper notch below for the workpiece to slide under it. Screw the fence to an L-shaped support board that hugs the side of the table, then clamp the support board to the table, making sure the blade fits into the end notch of the fence. Use strips of double-sided tape, as shown, to fasten each workpiece to the template, ensuring that the straight edges of the boards are aligned. Trim the workpiece if necessary to prevent it from hitting the fence when you make the cut.

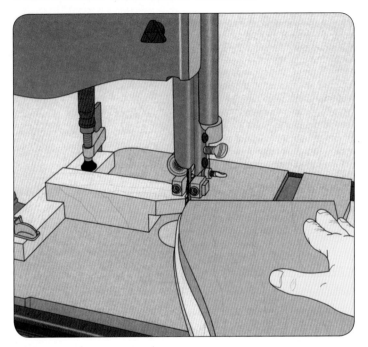

Lining up and starting the cut

Align the template and workpiece so that the edge of the template is parallel to the blade *(above).* To begin the cut, use your left hand to feed the workpiece into the blade. Once the blade begins cutting, apply slight pressure with your right hand to press the template squarely against the end of the double-point fence. Keep the template in contact with both points of the fence throughout the cut.

PATTERN SAWING *(continued)*

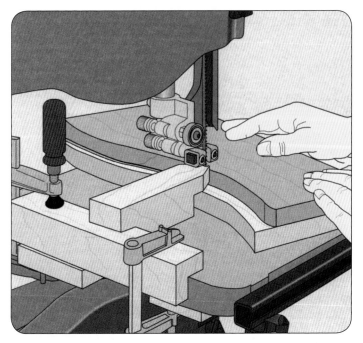

Completing the cut

Continue feeding with your left hand while using your right hand to keep the template flush against both points of the fence *(above)*; the template should ride along the fence as the blade cuts through the workpiece. Once you have finished the cut, pry the workpiece and template apart.

ROUNDING CORNERS

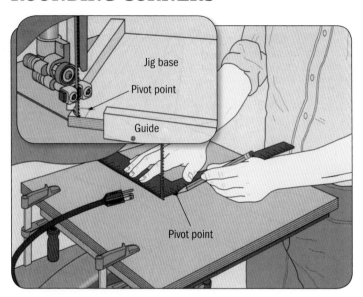

Setting up a quarter-circle-cutting jig

Cut a sheet of ¾-inch plywood slightly larger than the saw table, then feed it into the blade to cut a kerf from the middle of one side to the center. Clamp the sheet in position as an auxiliary table. Align a carpenter's square with the back of the blade gullets and mark a line on the auxiliary table that is perpendicular to the kerf. Then, mark a pivot point on the table the same distance from the blade as the radius of the rounded corners you plan to cut *(above)*. Cut another plywood sheet as a jig base and mark a square at one corner, with sides the same length as the radius of the rounded corners. Bore a hole for a screw at the marked corner (the spot marked "pivot point" on the inset illustration). Screw guides to adjacent edges of the jig base, then screw the jig base to the auxiliary table, centering the screw hole over the pivot point. Leave the screw loose enough to pivot the jig on the table. Round the marked corner of the jig by pivoting it into the blade *(inset)*.

ROUNDING CORNERS *(continued)*

Rounding a corner

To round the corner of a workpiece, turn off the saw and seat the workpiece against the guides of the jig. Turn on the saw, then use your right hand to pivot the jig, feeding the workpiece into the blade; your left hand should hold the workpiece snugly against the guides. Round each corner of a workpiece the same way *(above)*.

CUTTING A CREST RAIL

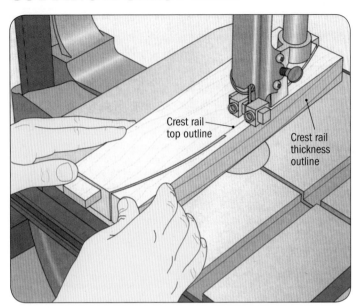

Crest rail top outline

Crest rail thickness outline

Cutting the top edge of the rail

Set the crest rail blank face-up on the band saw table, aligning the blade just to the waste side of the cutting line for the top of the rail. Feed the stock into the blade, turn off the saw about halfway through the cut, and remove the workpiece. Then cut along the same line from the opposite end. To avoid detaching the waste piece from the blank and losing the marked outline on the top edge of the rail, stop the cut about ¼ inch from the first kerf, leaving a short bridge between the two cuts (above).

CUTTING A CREST RAIL *(continued)*

Sawing the crest rail to thickness

Turn the rail blank so the marked outline on its top edge is facing up. Cut along both marked lines *(right)*. This time, complete the cut, letting the waste fall away. (This same cut is used to saw the back rail to thickness.)

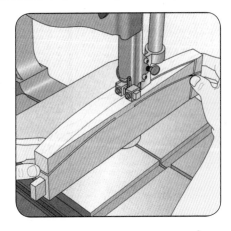

Severing the bridge

Rotate the crest rail blank so the first face you cut is facing up. With the saw turned off, feed the blade into the kerf. Then turn on the saw and cut through the bridge to release the waste piece *(right)*.

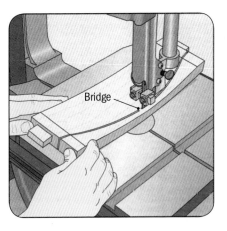

Bridge

MAKING CHAIR SLATS

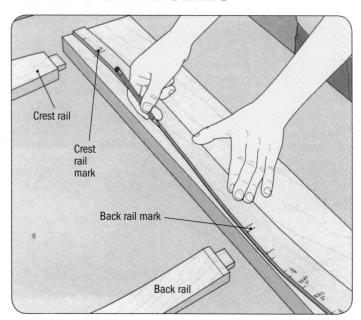

Crest rail

Crest
rail
mark

Back rail mark

Back rail

Determining the curve of the slats

Cut a blank wide enough to yield the number of slats you need for the chair. The thickness of the blank will determine the width of the slats, so make it 1 to 2 inches thick. Plan on producing an even number of slats so there will not be a single slat in the middle of the back rest exerting pressure on the chair user's spine. Mark the locations of the crest and back rails on the template, and add marks ½ inch beyond the first two to represent the ends of the slats that will fit into mortises in the rails. Next, place the template on the blank so the top ends are flush and mark the curve of the template on the blank with a pencil *(above)*. Then cut along your marked line on the band saw and smooth the cut edge.

Outlining the first slat

Transfer the slat end marks from the template to the blank. Then, with a pencil held between your thumb and index finger, run your middle finger along the curved edge of the blank to mark a cutting line parallel to the edge and ⅜ inch from it *(right)*. You can also use a marking gauge to scribe the cutting line.

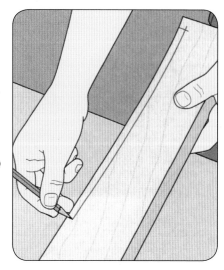

Cutting the first slat

Label the top and bottom ends of the slat, then cut the slat on the band saw *(right)*, keeping your hands well clear of the blade. Repeat to produce the number of slats you need.

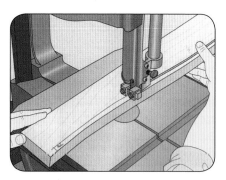

CIRCLE-CUTTING JIG

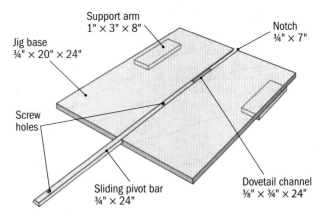

Support arm
1" × 3" × 8"

Notch
¾" × 7"

Jig base
¾" × 20" × 24"

Screw holes

Sliding pivot bar
¾" × 24"

Dovetail channel
⅜" × ¾" × 24"

For cutting perfect circles, use a shop-built circle-cutting jig custom-made for your band saw. Refer to the illustration above for suggested dimensions.

Rout a ⅜-inch-deep dovetail channel in the middle of the jig base, then use a table saw to rip a thin board with a bevel along two edges to produce a bar that slides smoothly in the channel. (Set the saw blade bevel angle by measuring the angle of the channel edges.) Cut out the notch on the band saw, then screw the support arms to the underside of the jig base, spacing them far enough apart to hug the sides of the band saw table when the jig is placed on it. Bore two screw holes through the bottom of the dovetail channel in the jig base 1 inch and 3 inches from the unnotched end; also bore two holes into the bar as shown.

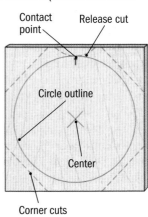

Contact point

Release cut

Circle outline

Center

Corner cuts

CIRCLE-CUTTING JIG *(continued)*

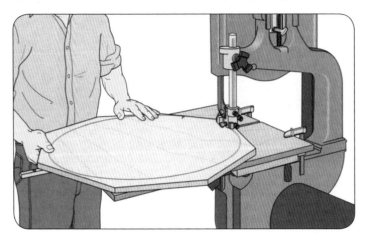

To prepare a workpiece for circle-cutting, mark the circumference and center of the circle you plan to cut on its underside *(left)*. Then, use the band saw to cut off the four corners of the workpiece to keep it from hitting the clamps that secure the jig to the table as the workpiece pivots. Make a release cut from the edge of the workpiece to the marked circumference, then veer off to the edge. Turn the workpiece over and mark the contact point where the blade touched the circumference.

Screw the narrow side of the bar to the center of the workpiece through one of the bar's holes. Do not tighten the screw; leave it loose enough to pivot the workpiece. Then, slide the bar into the channel and pivot the workpiece until the marked contact point is butted against the blade. Screw through one of the holes in the jig base to secure the pivot bar to the base.

To use the jig, pivot the workpiece into the blade *(above)*, feeding with your right hand and guiding with your left hand until the cut is completed.

CHAPTER 4:

Straight Cuts

With a depth of cut that can be extended to 12 inches on some machines, the band saw is the ideal shop tool for resawing. Whereas a 10-inch table saw would take two passes to resaw a 6-inch-wide board, a standard 14-inch band saw can make the same cut in a single pass.

Because the band saw blade is relatively thin, it produces a narrower kerf—and less waste—than is possible with a table or radial arm saw. The thin, flexible band saw blade has a natural tendency to sway from side to side imperceptibly as it cuts. You will need to keep your machine carefully tuned to get smooth and accurate cuts. Without such fastidious maintenance, crosscutting and ripping will be imprecise.

Band saw blades also have a tendency to "lead," or veer away from a straight line during a cut. This effect can be minimized by reducing feed speed and using sharp blades that are properly tensioned and tracked (*page 24*), though some lead is generally unavoidable. The lead of a particular blade is usually constant and predictable, so you can usually angle your rip fence to compensate for it.

Crosscutting is a safe procedure on the band saw. But remember, crosscutting is limited by the width of the throat: typically 10 to 14 inches on a two-wheel consumer-grade tool.

RIPPING

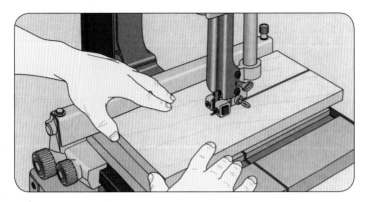

Ripping a board

Position the rip fence for the width of cut, adjusting its angle to compensate for blade lead. Butt the workpiece against the fence and feed it steadily into the blade with the thumbs of both hands *(above)*. To maintain proper control of the cut, straddle the fence with the fingers of your left hand and keep three fingers of your right hand braced on the table. Make sure that neither hand is in line with the blade.

*Shop*Tip

Compensating for blade lead
To set the angle of the rip fence and ensure accurate, straight cuts when using the rip fence as a guide, adjust the position of the fence on the saw table for each blade in the shop. Mark a cutting line on a board that is parallel to its edge. Then, cut halfway along the line freehand. You may have to angle the board slightly to keep the blade on the line; this is the result of blade lead. Mark a line on the table along the edge of the board. Align the rip fence parallel with this line whenever using the same blade.

A SHOP-MADE RIP FENCE

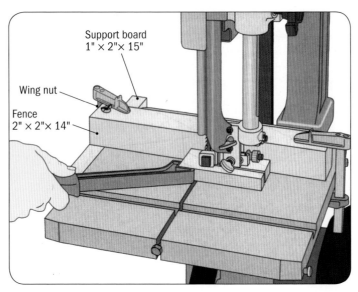

Support board
1" × 2"× 15"

Wing nut

Fence
2" × 2"× 14"

Like a commercial fence, the rip fence shown above can be adjusted to compensate for blade lead. First, fasten a wooden fence to a support board with a bolt and wing nut. The board should rest flush against the front edge of the saw table. Ensure that the fence will pivot when the wing nut is loosened.

To use the fence, first mark a line on the table for the blade lead *(page 61)*. Hold the support board in position, then loosen the wing nut to pivot the fence and align its edge with the marked line. Tighten the wing nut, then clamp the fence in place. Feed short or narrow stock, as shown, using a push stick.

A SHOP-MADE RIP FENCE *(continued)*

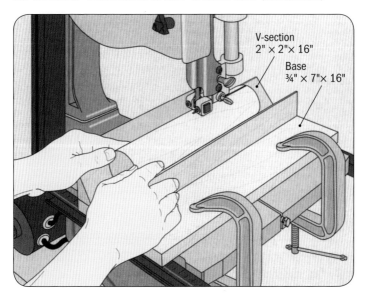

V-section
2" × 2"× 16"

Base
¾" × 7"× 16"

Ripping a cylinder

Rip a cylinder using a shop-made V-block jig. First, make the V section of the jig by bevel cutting a 2-by-2 diagonally. Then, screw the two cut pieces side-by-side to a base of solid wood or ¾-inch plywood to form a V. To provide clearance for the blade when using the jig, make a cut halfway across the center of the V and the base.

To make the rip cut, slip the blade through the clearance cut, then clamp the jig to the table. Feed the cylinder into the blade using the thumbs of both hands *(above)*. Keep your fingers away from the blade. For a cylinder that is too narrow to be cut through from the front of the table without endangering your thumbs, stop feeding midway through the cut. Then, move to the back of the table to pull the cylinder past the blade.

RESAWING

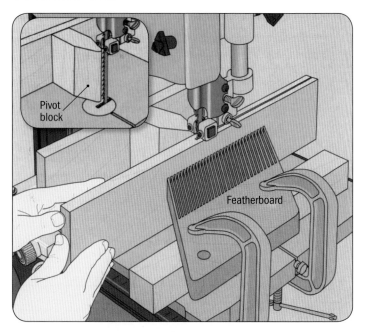

Pivot block

Featherboard

Using a pivot block and featherboard

To resaw a board, make a pivot block from two pieces of wood joined perpendicularly, with the shorter piece trimmed to form a rounded nose. Install the rip fence and screw the pivot block to it so the rounded tip is aligned with the blade *(inset)*. Position the rip fence for the width of cut and adjust its angle to compensate for blade lead *(page 61)*. To start the cut, feed the workpiece into the blade using the thumbs of both hands; use your fingers to keep the workpiece flush against the tip of the pivot block. A few inches into the cut, stop feeding and turn off the saw. Clamp a featherboard to the table, propping it on a wood scrap to support the middle of the workpiece. Turn on the saw and continue the cut *(above)* until your fingers reach the featherboard.

RESAWING *(continued)*

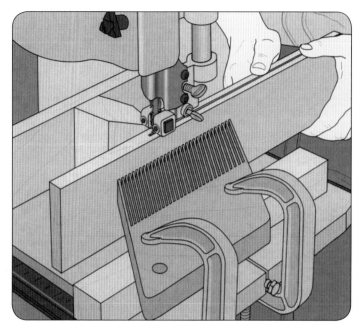

Completing the cut

With the saw still running, move to the back of the table to finish the cut. Use one hand to keep the workpiece square against the pivot block while pulling it past the blade with the other hand *(above)*.

SHOP-MADE VENEER

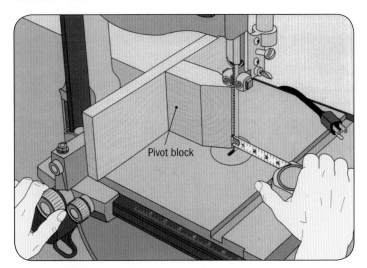

Pivot block

Setting up the cut

To cut veneer on the band saw, first make a pivot block from two pieces of wood joined in a T, with the outer end of the shorter piece trimmed to form a rounded nose. Install a ¾-inch resaw blade on the saw and install the rip fence on the table. Screw the pivot block to the fence so the rounded tip is aligned with the blade. Position the fence for the width of veneer you want *(above)*, typically ⅛ inch. If the stock you are cutting is relatively thin, clamp a featherboard to the table to support it during the cut.

SHOP-MADE VENEER *(continued)*

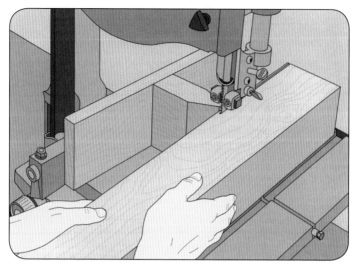

Cutting the veneer

Feed the workpiece into the blade with both hands, keeping the stock flush against the tip of the pivot block *(above)*. To prevent the blade from drifting off line, steer the trailing end of the workpiece. Near the end of the cut, move to the back of the table with the saw still running to finish the pass. Holding the stock square against the pivot block, pull it past the blade.

CROSSCUTTING

Using the rip fence as a guide

Position the rip fence for the length of cut, adjusting its angle to compensate for blade lead *(page 61)*. Butt the edge of the workpiece against the fence and feed it into the blade with the thumbs of both hands *(above)*. To maintain control of the cut, straddle the fence with the fingers of your left hand while keeping the fingers of your right hand braced on the face of the workpiece. Be sure that neither hand is in line with the blade.

Using the miter gauge as a guide

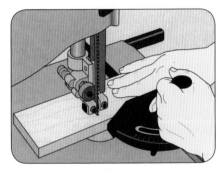

Use a carpenter's square to ensure that the miter gauge is perpendicular to the blade. Mark a cutting line on the leading edge of the workpiece. Holding the workpiece flush against the gauge, align the cutting line with the blade. With the thumb of your right hand hooked over the miter gauge, hold the workpiece firmly against the gauge and the saw table; use your left hand to push them together to feed the workpiece into the blade *(above)*. (Note: Do not try to compensate for blade lead when using the miter gauge for crosscutting.)

CROSSCUTTING *(continued)*

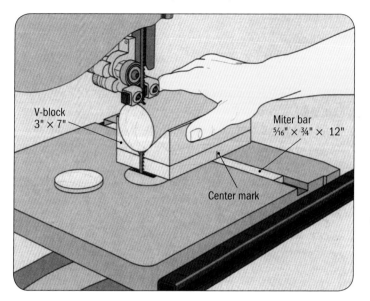

V-block
3" × 7"

Miter bar
$\frac{5}{16}$" × $\frac{3}{4}$" × 12"

Center mark

Crosscutting a cylinder

To crosscut a cylinder, make a V-block as described on page 63 but omitting the clearance cut. Butt the V-block against the blade and mark the center of the miter slot on the base of the V-block. Screw a narrow strip of wood to the bottom of the V-block to serve as a miter bar, aligning the screws with the center mark; countersink the screws to keep them from scratching the saw table when using the V-block. Glue a sandpaper strip to the inside edges of the V-block to keep the workpiece from slipping during the cut. Insert the miter bar into the miter slot and seat the workpiece in the V-block so it overhangs the edge of the V-block by an amount equal to the width of cut. Using your right hand to hold the workpiece firmly in the V-block, push it into the blade *(above)*.

ANGLE AND TAPER CUTS

By setting the band saw's miter gauge at an angle or tilting the saw table, you can make precise angle cuts, such as miters, bevels, and tapers. For a miter cut, use a sliding bevel to set the miter gauge to the desired angle—the gauge can be turned up to 90°—and then make the cut as you would a standard crosscut *(page 68)*. For best results, make a test cut, check the angle of the cut edge with a square and adjust the miter gauge setting, if necessary.

For a bevel cut, tilt the table to the desired angle—band saw tables tilt up to 45° to the right and 10° to the left—and, for a cut along the grain, install the rip fence on the right-hand side of the blade. This will position the workpiece on the "downhill" side of the blade, keeping the workpiece— and your hands—from slipping toward the blade for a safer cut. For more accurate cuts, adjust the angle of the rip fence to compensate for blade lead *(page 61)*. Then, cut the bevel as you would a standard rip cut. The simple setups shown below can be useful for making multiple miter and bevel cuts.

Taper cuts can be made freehand, but for several identical pieces, using a jig *(page 73)* guarantees uniform results.

MAKING REPEAT ANGLE CUTS

Mitering both ends of a board

Loosen the handle of the miter gauge and set the gauge to the desired angle. Then, screw a board to the gauge as an extension and cut off the end to the left of the saw blade. Glue a sandpaper strip to the extension to minimize the

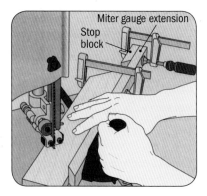

Miter gauge extension

Stop block

ANGLE AND TAPER CUTS *(continued)*

chance of the workpiece's slipping during a cut. Use the extension as a guide to cut the first miter, then make the miter cut on one end of a stop block. To cut the second miter, mark a cutting line on the leading edge of the workpiece. Holding the workpiece flush against the miter gauge, align the cutting line with the blade and butt the stop block against the end of the workpiece. Clamp the stop block and workpiece to the extension, then hook the thumb of your right hand over the miter gauge to hold the workpiece firmly against the gauge and the table. Use your left hand to feed the workpiece into the blade.

Cutting bevels

Loosen the table lock knobs and set the saw table to the desired angle. Screw a board to the miter gauge as an extension and cut off the end of it. Use the extension as a guide to cut the first bevel. To cut the second bevel, mark a cutting line on the leading edge of the workpiece.

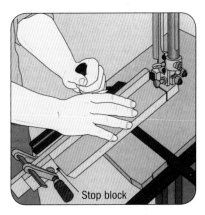

Stop block

Then, holding the workpiece flush against the miter gauge, align the cutting line with the blade and butt a stop block against the end of the workpiece. Clamp the stop block to the extension, then hook the thumb of your right hand over the miter gauge to hold the workpiece firmly against the gauge and the table. Use your left hand to push the miter gauge and workpiece together through the cut *(above)*.

MAKING TAPER CUTS

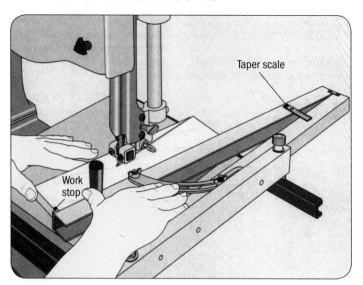

Taper scale

Work stop

Using a commercial taper jig

Install the rip fence to the right of the blade, then hold the taper jig
flush against the fence. Pivot the hinged arm of the jig until the taper
scale indicates the cutting angle—in degrees or inches per foot. Mark a
cutting line on the leading edge of the workpiece, then seat it against
the work stop and hinged arm. Position the fence so the cutting line on
the workpiece is aligned with the saw blade, then adjust the angle of the
fence to compensate for blade lead *(page 61)*. To make the cut, use the
thumbs of both hands to slide the workpiece and the jig as a unit across
the table, feeding the workpiece into the blade *(above)*. Use the fingers
of your left hand to hold the workpiece against the jig, ensuring that
neither hand is in line with the blade.

TAPER JIG

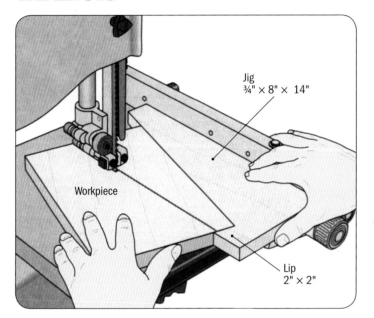

Jig
¾" × 8" × 14"

Workpiece

Lip
2" × 2"

Mark a line with the desired taper on the workpiece, then place the
workpiece on a board with a perfectly square edge, aligning the marked
line with the board's edge. Trace along the long edge of the workpiece
to mark an angled cutting line on the board. Saw along the cutting line
freehand, stopping 2 inches from the end of the cut at the bottom of the
board. Turn the board 90° to cut out the lip. To use the board as a jig, set
up the rip fence to the right of the blade, then hold the jig flush against
the fence. Align the edge of the jig's lip with the saw blade and lock the
fence in position, adjusting its angle to compensate for blade lead. Seat
the workpiece against the jig. Use the thumbs of both hands to slide the
workpiece and the jig as a unit across the table, feeding the workpiece into
the blade. Use the fingers of your left hand to hold the workpiece against
the jig, ensuring that neither hand is in line with the blade.

CHAPTER 5:
Cutting Duplicate Pieces

An effective method for producing multiple copies of the same shape is to fasten layers of stock together and cut the pieces in one operation with a technique known as stack sawing. Not only is it faster than cutting all the pieces separately; it also ensures that each piece is a precise copy of the original pattern. The method is possible because of the band saw's unique capacity to cut through very thick wood. With a 6-inch depth of cut, a band saw can cut through as many as eight pieces of ¾-inch plywood in a single pass.

To bond the layers of wood together in preparation for the cut, some woodworkers drive nails through the waste area; others use clamps. Both methods, however, can be hazardous if the blade accidentally strikes a nail or a clamp. A safer way is to use double-sided tape to hold the pieces together temporarily.

A stop block on the saw table will also save time when you are crosscutting repeatedly to turn out duplicate pieces. With the setup shown at right, you can speed the job of cutting a cylinder into identical slices.

TWO SETUPS FOR DUPLICATE PIECES

Stack sawing

Fasten the pieces together in a stack, then mark a cutting line on the top piece. Before turning on the saw, make sure that the blade is perfectly square with the saw table *(page 28)*; any error will be compounded from the top to the bottom of the stack. To cut the stack, first make any necessary release

Release cut

cuts *(page 47)*. For the curve shown, align the blade just to the waste side of the cutting line, then use the thumbs of both hands to feed the stack steadily along the marked path *(above)*. Keep your fingers on the edges of the stack and braced on the table to keep them safely away from the blade.

Using a stop block

Make a V-block with a miter bar as you would to crosscut a cylinder *(page 69)*. To produce several identical pieces, insert the V-block miter bar into the miter slot and clamp a stop block to the table so the distance between the stop block and the blade equals the desired cut-off length. For each cut, seat the workpiece in the V-block and butt

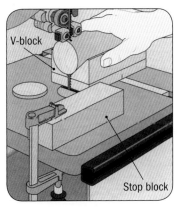

V-block

Stop block

it against the stop block. Using your right to hold the workpiece firmly in the V-block, push them together to feed the workpiece into the blade *(above)*.

HAND-SANDING JIGS

A Contoured Sanding Block

Plastic wrap

Making the block

To smooth the contours of a piece of molding, you can use a short sample of the molding to shape a sanding block that mates perfectly with the surface of the workpiece. Fashioning the block requires auto body filler or modeling rubber to make a mold of the profile. Start by nailing together a small box slightly larger than the sample molding and at least ¼ inch deeper than the thickest part of the molding. Prepare the filler following the manufacturer's instructions and fill about half the box with it. Lay a single thickness of plastic wrap over the box and, while the filler is still soft, press the molding sample into it *(above)* and clamp it firmly in place. Let the filler harden, then remove the molding sample from the box and

HAND-SANDING JIGS *(continued)*

the nails from the ends. Now saw off both ends of the box. Stretch a piece of sandpaper abrasive-side up across the molded side of the box. Use the molding sample to press the paper against the hardened filler, then staple the ends to the sides of the box *(left)*.

ShopTip

Sanding block
Cut a wood block that you can grip comfortably. On its top face, saw two narrow grooves and cut two wedge-shaped wood strips to fit in the gaps snugly. To provide even sanding pressure, you can glue a felt or cork pad to the bottom. Wrap a piece of sandpaper around the block, insert the ends into the grooves, then tap in the wedges to hold the paper in place.

CUTTING CIRCLES ON THE BAND SAW

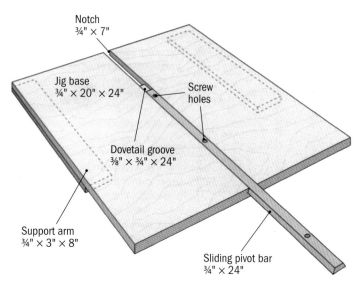

Notch
¾" × 7"

Jig base
¾" × 20" × 24"

Screw holes

Dovetail groove
⅜" × ¾" × 24"

Support arm
¾" × 3" × 8"

Sliding pivot bar
¾" × 24"

Building the jig

To cut perfect circles on the band saw, use a circle-cutting jig custom-built for your tool like the one shown above. Refer to the illustration for suggested dimensions. Use a router fitted with a dovetail bit to cut a ⅜-inch-deep groove in the middle of the jig base. Then use a table saw to rip a thin, beveled board that will slide smoothly in the channel. (Set the saw blade bevel angle by measuring the angle of the channel edges.) Cut out the notch on the band saw. Then position the jig base on the saw table so the blade lies in the notch and the dovetail groove is perpendicular to the direction of cut. Now screw the support arms to the underside of the jig base; the arms should hug the sides of the band saw table. Bore two screw holes through the bottom of the dovetail channel in the jig base roughly 1 inch and 3 inches from the unnotched end; also bore three holes through the bar.

CUTTING CIRCLES ON
THE BAND SAW *(continued)*

Preparing the workpiece

Mark the circumference and center of the circle you plan to cut on its underside. Then, use the band saw to cut off the four corners of the workpiece to keep it from hitting the clamps that will secure the jig to the table as the workpiece turns. Make a release cut from the edge of the workpiece to the marked circumference and veer off to the edge *(top right)*. Screw the pivot bar to the center of the workpiece through one of the bar's holes *(bottom right)*, leaving the screw loose enough to pivot the workpiece. Turn the workpiece over and mark the contact point where the blade touched the circumference during the release cut.

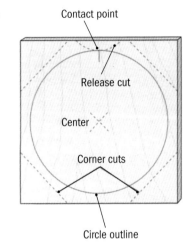

Contact point

Release cut

Center

Corner cuts

Circle outline

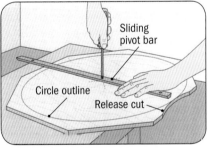

Sliding pivot bar

Circle outline

Release cut

CUTTING CIRCLES ON
THE BAND SAW *(continued)*

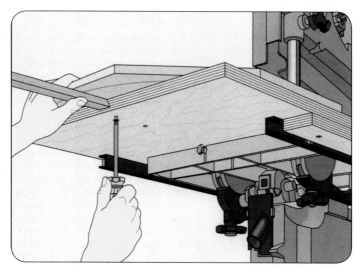

Securing the workpiece to the jig

Clamp the jig base to the band saw table, making sure the support arms are butted against the table's edges. Slide the pivot bar into the channel in the base and pivot the workpiece until the marked contact point touches the blade. Screw through one of the holes in the jig base to lock the pivot bar in place *(above)*.

CUTTING CIRCLES ON
THE BAND SAW *(continued)*

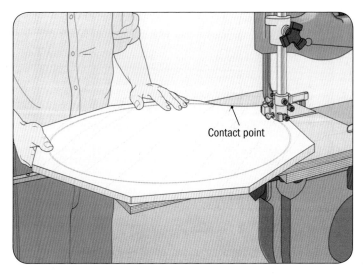

Contact point

Completing the circle

Turn on the saw and pivot the workpiece into the blade in a clockwise direction *(above)*, feeding the piece with your right hand until the cut is completed.

WEDGE-MAKING JIG

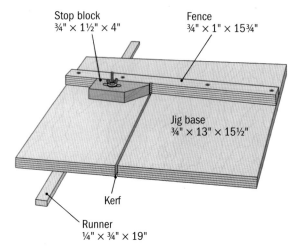

Stop block
¾" × 1½" × 4"

Fence
¾" × 1" × 15¾"

Jig base
¾" × 13" × 15½"

Kerf

Runner
¼" × ¾" × 19"

Building the jig

Small wedges are used for wedged tenons, or to shim cabinets on uneven floors. The jig shown above allows you to make them quickly on the band saw. (You can also use the same device on a table saw.) Refer to the illustration for suggested dimensions, making sure the hardwood runner fits snugly in the saw table miter slot. Screw the runner to the underside of the base so the runner extends beyond the tabletop and the base sits squarely on the table when the runner is in the slot; countersink the fasteners. Next, screw the fence to the top of the base; angle the fence at about 4° to the front and back edges of the base. Set the jig on the table with the runner in the slot, turn on the saw, and cut through the base until the blade contacts the fence. Turn off the saw, remove the jig, and cut a slot through the stop block for a machine bolt. Attach the block to the base, adding a washer and wing nut. The block should be flush against the fence with the tip of its angled end aligned with the kerf.

WEDGE-MAKING JIG *(continued)*

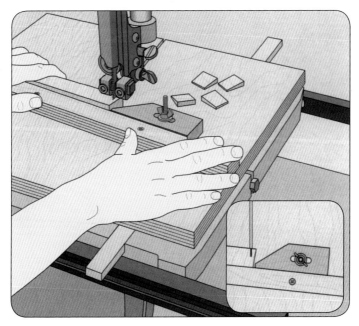

Cutting wedges

For your wedge stock, cut a strip of cross-grain wood from the end of a board; make it as wide as the desired length of the wedges. Position the jig on the saw table. Holding your stock with its edge flush against the fence and one end butted against the stop block, feed the jig across the table. Make sure your hands are clear of the blade as you cut each wedge *(above)*. To create 4° angle wedges, square the end of your stock on the table saw before each cut. If you simply flip the workpiece between cuts on the band saw, all the wedges after the first will have 8° angles. To produce thicker wedges, loosen the wing nut and slide the stop block slightly away from the kerf. Tighten the wing nut and cut the wedges *(inset)*.

TWO JIGS FOR ANGLE CUTS ON THE BAND SAW

Taper Jig

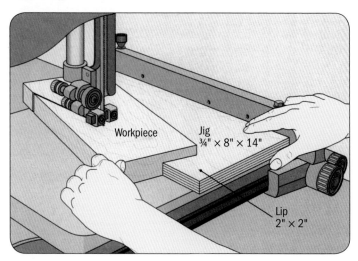

Workpiece

Jig
¾" × 8" × 14"

Lip
2" × 2"

Making taper cuts

The simple L-shaped jig shown at right will enable you to cut tapers on the band saw. Mark the desired taper on the workpiece and place it on a board with a perfectly square edge, aligning the marked line with the board's edge. Use the long edge and the end of the workpiece as a straightedge to mark an angled cutting line and the lip on the board. Saw along the cutting line, stopping 2 inches from the end of the cut at the bottom end of the board. Turn the board 90° to cut out the lip. To use the board as a jig, set up the band saw's rip fence to the right of the blade and hold the jig flush against the fence. Align the edge of the jig's lip with the saw blade and lock the fence in position. Seat the workpiece against the jig. Turn on the saw and slide the workpiece and the jig together across the table into the blade *(above)*, keeping both hands clear of the cutting edge.

TWO JIGS FOR ANGLE CUTS
ON THE BAND SAW *(continued)*

Miter Jig

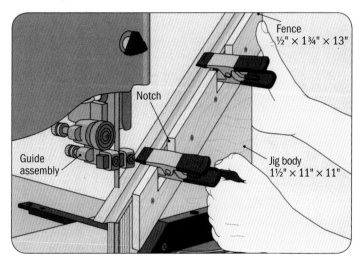

Labels on the image: Fence ½" × 1¾" × 13"; Notch; Guide assembly; Jig body 1½" × 11" × 11"

Mitering trim

Use the jig shown at left to miter trim on the band saw without angling the miter gauge. Form the jig body by face-gluing two square pieces of ¾-inch plywood together. Once the adhesive has dried, cut a 45° miter from corner to corner across the body, forming a ledge on which the workpiece will sit. Cut two slots into the face of the body ¼ inch below the angled ledge to accommodate spring clamp jaws. Next, cut the fence from solid stock, notch it for the clamps, and attach it to the jig body so its top edge extends ¼ inch above the ledge. Screw the jig to the miter gauge and feed the jig into the blade to trim the lower end. To cut a miter, clamp the workpiece face-down on the ledge and flush against the fence, and feed the jig toward with the miter gauge *(above)*. Be sure to raise the saw's guide assembly high enough to avoid hitting the jig or workpiece.

BUILDING AN EXTENSION TABLE FOR A BAND SAW

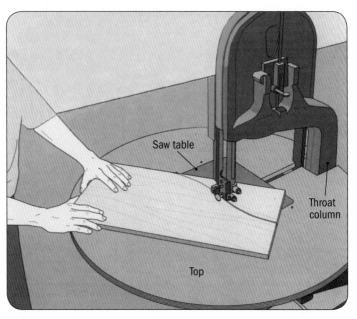

Saw table

Throat column

Top

An auxiliary band saw table will significantly increase the machine's versatility. The extension table shown above is especially handy for cutting long or wide pieces. Using ¾-inch plywood, cut the top of the jig to a suitable diameter. Cut out the center and the edge to fit the top around the saw table and throat column. Saw a 1½-inch-wide channel between the cutouts so the top can be installed without removing the blade. Next, prepare two cleats that will attach the saw table to the jig top. For these, two 1-by-3s should be cut a few inches longer than the saw table. Position each one in turn against the side of the saw table with threaded holes, so they are ¾ inch below the table surface, with at least ¼ inch of stock above the holes. (Make sure your machine has

BUILDING AN EXTENSION TABLE FOR A BAND SAW *(continued)*

Underside View   ### Overhead View

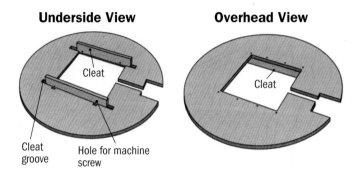

Cleat

Cleat

Cleat groove

Hole for machine screw

these holes; most band saws have them for mounting an accessory rip fence.) Depending on the position of the threaded holes on your saw table, you may have to position the top of the cleats closer than ¾ inch to the machine tabletop. In that case you will have to rout grooves for the cleats on the underside of the top to allow the tabletop to sit flush with the machine's table *(above, left)*. Mark the hole locations on the cleats, bore a hole at each spot, and fasten the cleats to the saw table with the screws provided for the rip fence. Then place the tabletop on the cleats and screw it in place *(above, right)*; be sure to countersink the screws. The top should sit level with the saw table. You may need to cut clearance notches so you can reach the machine screws once the jig is completed. To remove the jig, loosen only the machine screws, leaving the cleats attached to the top permanently.

Band Saw Joinery

A hallmark of fine craftsmanship, the dovetail joint is commonly used by cabinetmakers to join corners of better-quality drawers and casework.

The dovetail's interlocking pins and tails provide a joint that is not only strong and durable but also visually pleasing.

Cutting dovetail joints on the band saw offers advantages over using either hand tools or other power tools. For all the artistry and uniqueness of handcrafted dovetails, the hand-tool approach is a laborious process. And while

Dovetail joint

a router will make quick work of the job, it often produces pins and tails that are uniform in size and spacing. The result is a strong joint but one lacking in character.

Cutting dovetails on the band saw offers power-tool-type speed and precision. And as the following pages show, it is possible to tailor a dovetail joint on the band saw with the same flexibility you might bring to a handmade joint.

MAKING A DOVETAIL JOINT

Marking the pins

Outline the pins for the joint, following the sequence shown in the diagram at left. First, mark the outside face of each workpiece with a big X. Then, set a cutting gauge to the thickness of the stock and scribe a line all around the ends of the workpieces to mark the shoulder lines of the pins. Next, use a dovetail square to outline the pins on an end of one workpiece, starting with half-pins at each edge; you want the narrow sides of the pins to be on the outside face

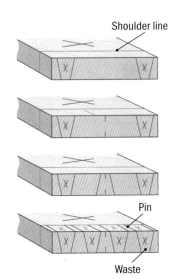

Shoulder line

Pin

Waste

of the workpiece. Outline the remaining pins *(right)*, marking the waste sections with an X as you go along. There are no rigid guidelines for spacing the pins of a dovetail joint, but spacing them fairly evenly, as shown, makes for a strong and attractive joint.

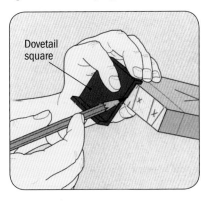

Dovetail square

MAKING A DOVETAIL JOINT *(continued)*

Making a Dovetail Joint

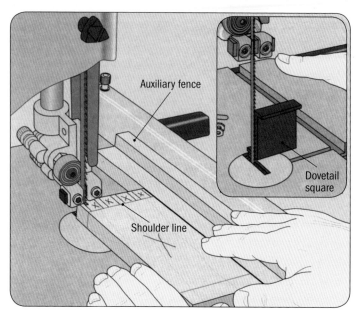

Auxiliary fence

Dovetail square

Shoulder line

Setting up the table and making the first cut

Cut one edge of each pin with the saw table tilted downward to the right.
To set up the table, loosen the lock knobs and set the table angle to
match the edge of the dovetail square *(inset)*, then tighten the lock knobs.
Set up the rip fence and screw a wooden L-shaped auxiliary fence to
it. Then, with the workpiece on the saw table outside-face up, align the
marked line for the right-hand edge of the first half-pin with the saw blade.
Butt the auxiliary fence against the workpiece. To make the cut, feed the
workpiece into the blade using the thumbs of both hands *(above)*; press
the workpiece flush against the auxiliary fence with your left hand and
straddle the fence with your right hand. Stop the cut and turn off the saw
when the blade reaches the shoulder line on the face of the workpiece.

MAKING A DOVETAIL JOINT *(continued)*

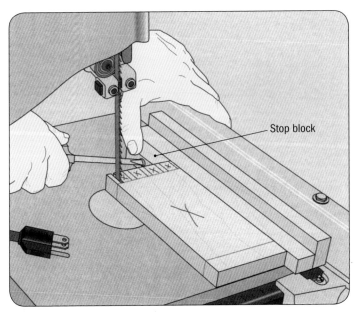

Stop block

Using a stop block for repeat cuts

With the blade butted against the shoulder line, hold a stop block against the workpiece and screw it to the auxiliary fence *(above)*. To cut the right-hand edge of the first half-pin at the other end of the workpiece, rotate the workpiece 180° and hold it flush against the auxiliary fence. Then make the cut the same way you cut the first half-pin, stopping when the workpiece touches the stop block. Rotate the workpiece 180° again, align the blade with the marked line for the right-hand edge of the next pin, butt the auxiliary fence against the work-piece, and cut to the stop block. Continue, shifting the position of the rip fence as necessary and cutting the right-hand edge of each pin on both ends of the workpiece.

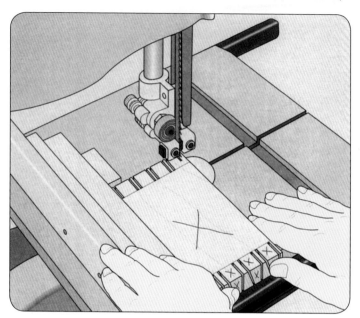

Cutting the pins' left-hand edges

Cut the left-hand edge of each pin with the table tilted downward to the left. Use the dovetail square to set the table angle; remove the table stop, if necessary. Install the rip fence to the left of the blade and screw the auxiliary fence to it. Then cut the left-hand edges of the pins the same way you cut the right-hand edges. Next, use a chisel to remove the waste between the pins. With the workpiece outside-face up on a work surface, strike the chisel with a wooden mallet to cut through the wood just to the waste side of the shoulder line. Hold the chisel square to the end of the workpiece to split off each waste section in thin layers. Remove about one-half of each section, then turn the workpiece over to remove the other half. Finally, pare the edges of the pins with the chisel.

MAKING A DOVETAIL JOINT *(continued)*

Outlining the tails

Set the tail board outside-face down on a work surface. Then, holding the pin board end-down on the tail board with its outside face away from the tail board, align the pins with the end of the tail board. Use a pencil to mark the outline of the tails on the ends of each tail board *(right)*, then mark the waste pieces.

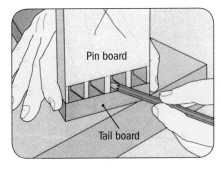

Pin board

Tail board

Cutting the tails

Return the table to the horizontal position to cut out the waste between the tails. Cut the waste beside the half-tails at the edges of the workpiece with two intersecting cuts. For waste between tails, nibble at the waste with the blade, pivoting the workpiece as necessary to avoid cutting into the tails *(right)*. Test-fit the joint and make any necessary adjustments with a chisel.

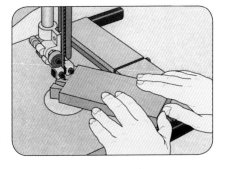

DOVETAILED HALF-LAP JOINTS

Combining the strength of the dovetail joint with the simplicity of the half-lap, the dovetailed half-lap is a favorite joinery method for frames and table stretchers. The joint strongly resists tension.

MAKING A DOVETAILED HALF-LAP JOINT

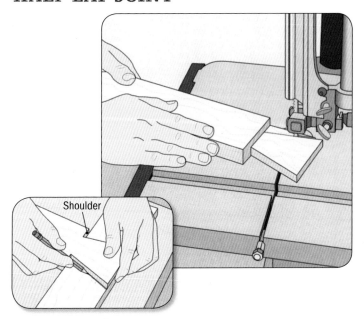

Shoulder

Cutting the dovetailed half-lap and the socket

In one workpiece, cut a corner half-lap. Then, outline the dovetail on the cheek of the half-lap and cut it out on the band saw *(right)*; use an angle of 1:8 if you are working with hardwood, or a 1:6 angle for softwood. Use the dovetailed half-lap to outline the socket in the mating workpiece; make sure the shoulder of the half-lap is butted against the edge of the board as you mark the lines *(left)*. Make the socket using a router with a template, a table saw, a radial arm saw, or a handsaw and miter box, cutting to one-half the stock thickness.

KNUCKLE JOINTS

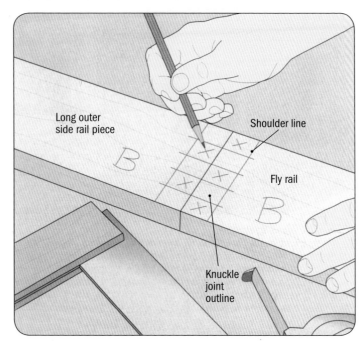

Long outer side rail piece

Shoulder line

Fly rail

Knuckle joint outline

Preparing the side rails

Butt the mating ends of a fly rail and the long outer side rail piece
together, making sure the board edges are aligned. Use reference letters
to label the pieces, then mark a shoulder line on each board about
one inch from their mating ends; use a try square to ensure the lines are
perpendicular to the board edges. To complete the joint outline, use a
tape measure to divide the boards into five equal segments across their
width, creating a grid of fingers and notches on the board ends. Mark
the waste sections—or notches—with Xs *(above)* so the fly rail will have
three notches and the mating piece two notches.

KNUCKLE JOINTS *(continued)*

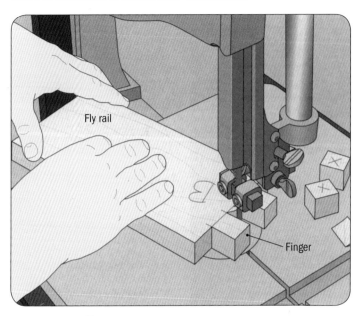

Fly rail

Finger

Sawing the fingers

To cut the fingers at the end of the fly rail on your band saw, start by sawing out the waste at both edges of the piece with two intersecting cuts. To clear the waste between the fingers, nibble at it with the blade, pivoting the piece as necessary to avoid cutting into the fingers *(above)*. Once all the fingers are cut, test-fit the joint and make any necessary adjustments with a chisel.

CUTTING THE FLY RAILS TO LENGTH

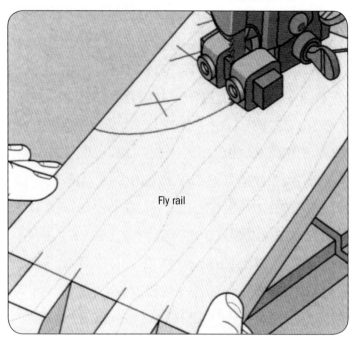

Fly rail

Refer to the anatomy illustration *(page 96)* to mark the S-shaped cutting line on the fly rails, then designate the waste with Xs. Feed the stock across the band saw table *(above)*, making certain neither hand is in line with the blade. Make matching cuts on the mating ends of the short outer rail pieces, ensuring that there will be a sufficiently large gap—about ½ inch—between the two boards for handhold.

CUTTING THE CURVED FACE OF AN END RAIL

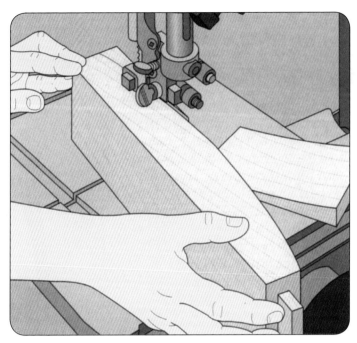

Outline the curved outside face of the end rail on the edges so the legs will extend ¼ inch beyond the rail when the table is assembled. Then, standing at the side of the band saw table, set the rail down on edge. Align the blade just to the waste side of the cutting line, near the center, and hold the two ends to feed the stock across the table; make sure neither hand is in line with the blade. Once one waste piece falls away, turn the rail over and cut the opposite end *(above)*.

Cabriole Legs

MAKING A CABRIOLE LEG

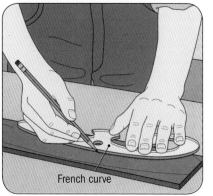

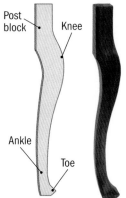

Despite its delicate appearance, a cabriole leg provides excellent strength. A well-balanced leg should be able to stand by itself.

Post block

Knee

Ankle

Toe

Designing the leg

For a template, cut a piece of stiff cardboard or hardboard to the same length and width as your leg blanks. The design shown above will yield a stable and well-proportioned leg, but you can alter the design to suit your project. Begin drawing the leg by outlining the post block. Make its length equal to the width of the rail that will be attached to it; the post block should be wide enough to accept the rail tenons. Next, sketch the

MAKING A CABRIOLE LEG *(continued)*

toe and the front of the leg from the toe to the ankle using a French curve; at its narrowest point, the ankle should measure about two-fifths of the stock width. Move on to the knee, sketching a gentle curve from the post block to the front edge of the template about 3 to 4 inches below the block. Then join the knee to the ankle with a relatively straight line. Complete the outline at the back of the leg, connecting the bottom of the leg with the back of the ankle, then sketching a curve from the ankle to the bottom of the post block. You may need to redraw the curves several times until you are satisfied with the design.

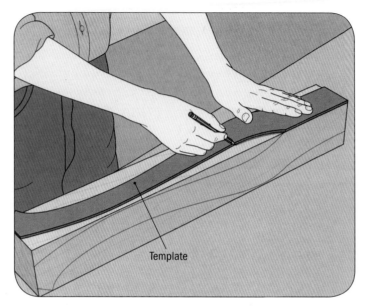

Template

Transferring the design

Cut out your template on a band saw, then sand the edges to the
marked outline. To trace the outline on the leg blank, place the template
flat on one of the inside faces of the blank, making sure that the ends
of the template and the blank are aligned and that the back of the post
block is flush with the inside edge of the blank. Trace along the edges
of the template. Turn the blank over and repeat the procedure on the
other inside face *(above)*. At this point, some woodworkers prefer to cut
mortises or drill holes for the leg-to-rail joinery. (It is easier to clamp
and cut joints on a rectangular leg blank than on a leg with pronounced
curves.) Other woodworkers cut the leg first and then do the joinery.

MAKING A CABRIOLE LEG (continued)

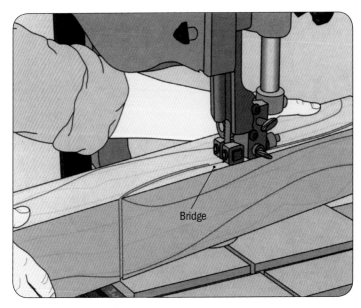

Bridge

Cutting out the leg

Set the leg blank on the band saw table with one of the outlines facing up and the toe of the leg pointing away from you. Aligning the saw blade just to the waste side of the marked line for the back of the leg, feed the stock into the cutting edge. Turn off the saw about halfway through the cut and remove the blank. Then cut along the same line from the opposite end. To avoid detaching the waste piece from the

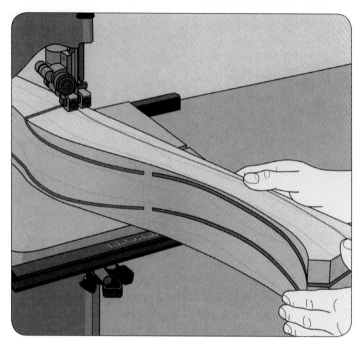

blank and losing the marked outline on the adjacent face, stop the cut about ½ inch from the first kerf, leaving a short bridge between the two cuts *(opposite page)*. Retract the workpiece, then cut along the line for the front of the leg, again leaving bridges. Turn the blank and saw along the marked lines on the adjacent side *(above)*. This time, complete the cut, letting the waste fall away.

MAKING THE CUTS ON
THE ADJACENT FACE

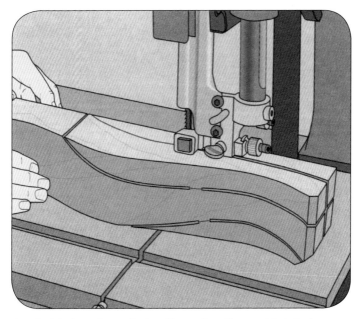

Turn the blank so the marked outline on its adjacent side is facing up.
Cut along the marked lines, beginning at the foot *(above)*. This time,
complete the cuts, letting the waste pieces fall away.

MAKING THE CUTS ON
THE ADJACENT FACE *(continued)*

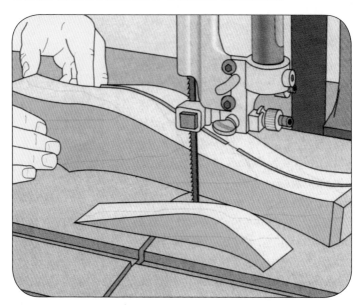

Cutting the bridges

Rotate the blank so the first face you cut faces up. With the saw off, slide the blank forward to feed the blade into the kerf at the back of the leg. Turn on the saw and cut through the bridge to release the waste piece *(above)*. Then cut through the bridge between kerfs at the back of the leg.

SHAPING AND SMOOTHING THE LEG

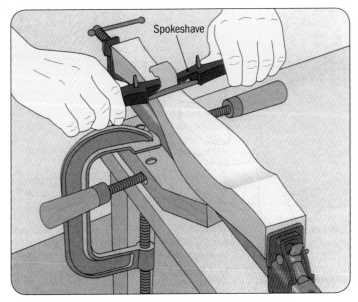

Spokeshave

To finish shaping a cabriole leg and to remove any blemishes left by the band saw blade, smooth its surfaces with a spokeshave, followed by a rasp and sandpaper. Secure the leg in a bar clamp and fix the clamp to a work surface with a handscrew and C clamp as shown. Holding a spokeshave with both hands at the top of a curved edge of the leg, pull the tool slowly toward you, cutting a thin shaving and following the grain *(above)*. Repeat until the surface is smooth. Turn the leg in the bar clamp to clean up the other edges. Use the rasp to smooth an area that the spokeshave cannot reach. The tool works best when pushed diagonally across the grain. Finish the job with sandpaper, using progressively finer-grit papers until the surface is smooth.

Index

Index

INDEX

Back to **Basics**

Straight Talk for Today's **Woodworker**

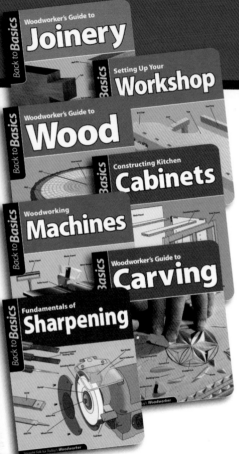

Woodworker's Guide to Joinery
ISBN 978-1-56523-462-8
$19.95 • 192 Pages

Setting Up Your Workshop
ISBN 978-1-56523-463-5
$19.95 • 152 Pages

Woodworker's Guide to Wood
ISBN 978-1-56523-464-2
$19.95 • 160 Pages

Constructing Kitchen Cabinets
ISBN 978-1-56523-466-6
$19.95 • 144 Pages

Woodworking Machines
ISBN 978-1-56523-465-9
$19.95 • 192 Pages

Woodworker's Guide to Carving
ISBN 978-1-56523-497-0
$19.95 • 160 Pages

Fundamentals of Sharpening
Coming Winter 2011

Get *Back to Basics* with the core information you need to succeed. This new series offers a clear road map of fundamental woodworking knowledge on sixteen essential topics. It explains what's important to know now and what can be left for later. Best of all, it's presented in the plain-spoken language you'd hear from a trusted friend or relative. The world's already complicated – your woodworking shouldn't be.